So, You Really Want a Horse!

by

Janet E. Dzurnak

DORRANCE PUBLISHING CO., INC.
PITTSBURGH, PENNSYLVANIA 15222

ISBN # 0-8059-4398-6
Printed in the United States of America

First Printing

For information or to order additional books, please write:
Dorrance Publishing Co., Inc.
643 Smithfield Street
Pittsburgh, Pennsylvania 15222
U.S.A.

This book is dedicated to the memory of my many wonderful equine friends and teachers. Each one was a professor in his or her own way.

"COMMANDER"
the very first horse I got to know. He was assigned to me to groom and tend, feed and learn from. He taught me to ride. His patience and caring helped nurture my love for horses in the very beginning when I was just six years old.

"ROCKY"
who stood for hours while I just talked to him and groomed him. I spent my teen years in his care. He helped me develop that wonderful trust for the horse's sense of quiet caring.

"CISCO"
my first horse. I had never been able to call a horse "mine" before him. He introduced me to the wonders of trail riding and nature. He taught me to care for a horse—grooming, nursing, and feeding.

"EL GHATO"
He showed me that there are crazy mean horses in the world. He let me know that (as with people) you cannot trust all horses. He proved that horses can hurt and will be mean or unpredictable.

"COMANCHE WARRIOR"

my beloved POO BEAR. He showed me the beauty of openhearted unselfish love. He helped me experience the wonder of horses, inside and out. He taught me patience, kindness, trust, gentleness, and ever-lasting faith. His heart was bigger than his whole body. He loved me and trusted me completely. He was totally devoted and returned three-fold every kindness given him. He introduced me to the fabulous Morgan horse.

CONTENTS

A special thanks to my present wonderful fourfooted friends whom I love dearly. They are my true friends and very special people.

"BANDIT," "BEAU," and "DARBY."

God Bless you, Buddy.

To the following horses I give my heartfelt thanks for all their giving and understanding. Most of them spent many years in my stable and in my care. They each taught me something precious in their own way. It was a pleasure knowing and working with every one of them. They were the teachers—I was the student. They all have their own special place in my world of memories.

"TIPPY PALOUSE," "SIOUX," "ROANY," "JIM BUNN," "APACHE," "TRINIDAD," "BARNEY," "AARIAL," "TRADER," "MARIAH," "AMOS," "NETTY," "TJ," "DAISY," "RED," "SONNY," "NARISSA," "STAR."

I WOULD LIKE TO TAKE THIS OPPORTUNITY TO THANK THE SPECIAL PEOPLE WHO ADVISED ME TO TAKE THE CHANCE ON PUBLISHING THIS BOOK. I THANK THEM FOR THEIR KIND ADVICE, THEIR CONSTRUCTIVE CRITICISM, AND THE MANY HOURS THEY SPENT PROOFREADING MY WORK.

THANK YOU, JUDY AND PAT, MY GOOD FRIENDS AND TRAIL BUDDIES.

THE HORSE

Here is nobility without conceit,
friendship without envy, beauty without vanity,
a willing servant, yet no slave.

INTRODUCTION

So, you really want a horse.

You dream about horses, play like horses, eat, drink and sleep horses. You talk about nothing else. You beg for one for your birthday, pray for one for Christmas. You tell Mom how you can keep it in the garage. She'll have good manure for her roses. You will take such good care of it that no one will know it's there!

Your bedroom walls are plastered with posters and pictures of horses, colts, Clydesdales, ponies. You run around in jeans, ride your wild imaginary stallion, and groom him by the hour. There's that old worn out bridle you bought at a garage sale for two dollars, that rusty horseshoe you found in the park and brought home. You pretend it came off your own horse. Horse statues are tucked in every corner.

If Mom and Dad would just understand how good you would be, you would never let them down. The horse would be no trouble. You promise! You will work odd jobs to pay for him and do all the work yourself . . . If . . .

Does that sound familiar? That's how I grew up. From the time I was six or seven, my every waking thought had four hoofs, a mane, a tail, and me on his back. I pictured us floating together as one motion. My horse! I spent all day at the nearby riding stable grooming horses and cleaning stalls or tack just so I could ride for one hour. All my friends were playing with dolls, learning to cook and take care of children. Girls wanted to be teachers or mothers! The farthest things from my mind were boys and babies!

Now I am fifty-five years old. I was through school and married when I finally got my first horse. He was ten months old when we brought him home, and I had him until he was twenty-five years old. I have another horse now; he will be eighteen this year. I look back over the years of sweat, fun, work, play, and—don't forget—PAIN. Here are the cold, hard, unflowered facts about owning a horse. It is worth it, but IT IS WORK! It is about 85 percent work and 15 percent riding and fun. Horses are truly one of **GOD's** greatest gifts to man. They not only

1

did his work, fought his wars, and carried him all over the world, but they are beautiful and faithful and can be very loving and understanding. **GOD** *FORBID THAT I SHOULD EVER GO TO A HEAVEN WHERE THERE ARE NO ANIMALS,* especially horses and dogs.

So, you really want a horse? Let's explore that question together. Sit back, relax, and here we go . . .

I headed down to the barn to feed for the evening. I had been in the barn earlier. I had turned the horses out, cleaned the stalls, and generally gone over the barn dusting and whatever. I had put the horses back in their stalls and gone back up to the house.

When I returned to the barn, everything was unusually quiet. This is not normal. I am usually greeted with hungry nickers or some kind of noise. When I entered the aisleway I could not see Comanche. He is usually right there at the front of his stall to greet me. I walked over to the stall and looked in over the wall. He was laying in the corner all twisted, with his feet up in the air against the wall. Oh GOD! I had heard about horses becoming cast, but I had never seen it before. He looked pathetic. He was covered completely with foam—as if he had been sprayed with shaving cream. This was his own sweat. He must have been in terrible pain! I opened the door and approached him. He was always so good to treat when he was ill, he trusted people completely, knowing they would help him.

When I entered the barn and he heard my voice, he must have stopped his struggling, for he was absolutely quiet. As I walked up to him he gave me the most beseeching and pathetic look, as if to say, "Please help me. Make it stop hurting." I talked to him and calmed him down. I could feel and see him relax. He knew I would help somehow. But how? I had no idea what to do. I put his halter on and talked to him gently and calmly, knowing I had to keep him quiet. I knew I had to remain calm and not panic. He drew his strength from me. If I panicked now, he would, too. He began to relax a little.

Then I left him and went to the phone. I had to get help. I called my husband at work. He suggested that I call our neighbor for help. I called the neighbor, and she sent over her stable helper to see what he could do. With his help we managed to roll Comanche over so he could get his feet under him and get up. He stood teetering until he got his balance. Then he seemed to get his strength back. The neighbor suggested I call my vet right away. I left the horse in his care while I did this.

I explained to the vet how I had found him and what I did. He suggested that I walk him as long as I could and not let him lay down or try to roll. He was probably suffering from colic. He asked what the horse had done that day. I told him that he was out in the corral for two hours while I cleaned stalls. He asked me what he could have eaten. It was then I remembered the apple trees and suggested that he may have eaten ground apples. He suggested that I get some oil into him and walk him until he had two or more bowel movements. The vet also told me to keep him posted.

The neighbor left after I talked to the vet. He said to call again if I needed more help. I thanked him. Now I began walking. For two, maybe three hours we walked. I talked to him, groomed him, joked with him, anything I could do to keep him interested in me and not his hurting belly. He finally had one then another bowel movement. He began to move more easily and look better. By the time I was done, he was spotlessly clean. I had groomed all the sweat off him, even his mane and tail. He was feeling much better, and I was dog tired. Between worrying and walking, I was worn out.

I will never forget green-apple colic. I had heard about it. Now I understood it. Now I knew what it was to have a horse cast. I knew what colic was and how it hurt. It causes a horse to lay down and roll. They roll to relieve the pain—gas pain. It is the only thing they can think of to stop the hurt. The only thing is, rolling can increase the pain by causing the intestine to twist—what they call a "torsion". This can be deadly. Colic can kill a horse very quickly if not handled properly. It was lucky for me that Comanche got hung up halfway over and could not go any farther. He had to lay there in pain and wait for me to come. That is why he was so covered with foamy sweat. This was lucky for both of us because he could have twisted his intestines and died. The only cure for a twisted intestine is surgery. Here in Ohio that is performed at Ohio State University. That is a two hour drive from where I live. Some horses make it, some don't. It's a long ride to make in so much pain. I could have lost my best friend that day. I was very lucky. We have been through a lot together. I have made a lot of mistakes. He has been very forgiving. I have learned from these mistakes. Luckily, none of them have been too terrible. I have become a better person for them.

THE DREAM AND THE TRUTH

THE WAY YOU ALWAYS DREAM IT WILL BE:

Your dream horse: Name: Sun Dancer
                  Sex: Gelding
                  Age: Five years old
                  Breed: Quarter horse
                  Color: Bright chestnut with blaze
                  Size: 15.2 hands

It's a beautiful day, and all you can think about is riding. You get dressed, eat a light breakfast, and head for the barn. When you get there your horse calls out his soft greeting as soon as he hears you. There he is, sparkling clean, just waiting for you. You saddle up, mount, ride, and enjoy exploring the world together for the next few hours. You relish the sunshine, the wildlife, and most of all, each other's company. Just you and your horse.

You reluctantly return to the barn, tired but content, and take off his saddle and bridle. You rub him down, clean him up, and pat his neck. Then you put him in his stall, stuff a carrot in his mouth, hang up your tack, and leave.

That's just how you think about it, right? Exactly how it should be, right? Well, let's change the picture a little. Let's add a word called ***REALITY!***

THE WAY IT REALLY HAPPENS:

Your real horse: Name: Clod Hopper
                 Sex: Gelding
                 Age: Nine years, I think. (I was told he was seven when I bought him. That puts him between seven and twelve)

Breed:	Plain brown horse!
Color:	Brown (or whatever he sheds out to in the spring), white blaze, and one white sock when it's clean.
Size:	15.1 hands, I think. (He won't stand still to be measured!)

It's morning. You peek your head out from the covers, and by gosh, the sun is shining! There are so many things you would like to do if only you weren't so tired and sore. You've been working late to get in some overtime, and you slept rotten last night. Oh well, let's get up!

Gee, it would be a nice day to ride. You have so many other things to do. Yet, you have to get out to that barn. It's been raining off and on for the past five days. You have to get him out before he tears the barn apart. He's going to be rank. His stall is a mess, and you have to clean it. That was the agreement so you could save money. You clean your own stall. Just hope the corral isn't too muddy when you turn him out. If he rolls in that mud, you'll never get him clean enough to ride. You had to get a horse that likes to roll!

Oh well. Off to the barn after gulping down a cup of tea and a piece of toast. You get to the barn, and he greets you with a loud whinny, as if to say, "It's about time!" When you open the door you see a loose board. Great! Have to repair that. Slip the halter on and turn him out. Oh, the mud! While he has fun sliding in the mud, you proceed to fix the stall board.

After an hour's time, the stall is clean. The water bucket has been removed and scrubbed, the loose board repaired, and a check made for loose nails. Everything is in order inside. Now for the horse. He comes willingly for a change—you don't have to bribe or chase him. But what a mess! He rolled in the muddiest places he could find. He even has mud between his ears! Thanks a lot! Sometimes you feel he does it on purpose just to get back at you. Nevertheless he really enjoyed it. Down deep you know you're glad because he really needed to kick up his heels and just be a horse. Now back to work.

Starting with a sweat scraper, you remove most of the dirt and mud. Then, with a shedding blade, you proceed to loosen and remove most of the shedding winter coat. By golly, there's a horse under there! With all the rubbing and scrubbing, you have him practically falling over in pure delight. How he loves a rubdown. Progress is being made. Next the curry loosens the rest of the hair and dirt. Finally, a good brushing. An hour and a half later you have a really decent-looking horse. He thoroughly enjoyed it, too. Too bad you are so dirty and sweaty. No one ever told you this was a clean job. Besides, you're here. You might as well ride. You really could use the fun after all the work.

You brush yourself off, rinse your hands and face a little, and head for the tack room. Upon close inspection you notice that your cinch is bad. Now where did you put that extra cinch? You also forgot to bring the clean saddle pad you had taken home to wash. Well, you'll just get by with the old one today. Besides, the horse is too dirty for a clean pad. There, finally he's saddled and bridled, and you are ready to go. One quick look at the watch. You're running late, but you really do need this ride. Off you go.

Down trail everything is great. When you are here you always wonder why you don't take more time away from everything to ride and be with your horse. You have such a great relationship. He asks so little—just that you care—and he cares when everyone else turns you away. He doesn't care if you are ten pounds overweight or have a "bad hair day" or don't drive the best car and wear the latest fashions. He doesn't even care if you forgot to brush your teeth and have bad breath! He loves you for what you are, not for what you should be. Everything is so peaceful when you are down trail or in the barn. All those nagging problems seem so far away. All the work is really worth it after all. This is better than a tranquilizer. Ought to name your horse Tylenol® or Valium®!

Then today Jughead decides he doesn't want to cross the river. For fifteen to twenty minutes there is a battle of wits. Finally, when you are just about ready to give up, he takes a flying leap right into the middle of the river, sending a tidal wave in all directions. You are both drenched! At first you are angry, then you just sit there and laugh. That's why you love him so much. He's such an unpredictable NUT! The rest of the ride is great, peaceful with no unusual happenings.

You look at your watch. Oh boy, it's really getting late! So you pick up the gait and head back. It's always amazing how long it takes to go out and how short the ride back is. It is warmer than you thought, and the horse gets sweaty. After you strip off the gear, you know you have to cool him down. Get out the bucket and sponge. Put a little liniment into the water. A gentle sponge bath works wonders. The liniment helps to cool him down as well as work on sore muscles. In a few minutes he is cool and clean. A quick spray of Show Sheen on his legs and sides will help to keep him clean—especially since he likes to roll. Now a touch up here and there with a brush, and, finally, the feet.

You start picking out the feet. Oh great, he has a nice chip here. Get the rasp and file that down before it leads to trouble. The farrier isn't due for another two weeks. The other three feet aren't too bad, but he has a touch of thrush in one. Treat that. Now oil them really well and you can put him away. Be sure to give him his treats before you go. Got to get home, clean up, and run the rest of the errands for the day. Don't want to go around smelling like horse sweat and manure. People look at you funny.

WELL, THAT'S THE WAY IT REALLY IS. Not quite as glamorous as the first picture and quite a bit more to take into consideration.

THINK SERIOUSLY

I am not writing this to discourage anyone from owning a horse. I am simply asking you to think and consider. A horse is a very sensitive animal. They pull an awful lot of strength and happiness from their owners. They need love, affection, and consideration just as much as another person or your pet dog. However, they do give in return.

They have many feelings. If you pay attention to another horse before saying hello to them, they feel jealous or neglected. If you ignore them, they feel hurt or angry. If you haven't been to the barn for a while due to illness or vacation, they miss you, even pine for you. Another person may exercise them and feed them, but they miss you! They become very attached to their owners. Even if their owners neglect them.

The after-ride ritual is the part I probably enjoy more than anything. I just enjoy being around my horse and doing for him. After the ride, the horse is content. He's had his exercise, he's gotten out all his little bucks and kinks, and now he just wants to be cared for. My horse is especially loving and appreciative of all I do for him. He will nuzzle, rub, and touch just like a kitten. The after-ride time is when he is really in tune with me and what I do for him. I have known him to put his head over my shoulder and draw me into his chest as if he were giving me a hug.

I am one of the few horse people I know of who likes working around the horse and barn equal to riding or almost better than. I do not like arena riding. To me it is boring. Why would anyone like looking at four walls all the time? I don't understand this. Nevertheless, some people prefer this. I am a trail rider. I did not have access to an arena without paying for its use until just recently. My husband and I finally broke down and put up our own arena. We board and care for eight other horses, and the people need an arena, especially when they work all day and can only ride on the weekends or at night. They also need a place to exercise their animals when the weather is bad. Now, finally, I have a place to work my horse when the weather is bad. I never used to. I must admit it is the first time my horse has never been out of condition. Even when the weather was bad and I could not ride, I enjoyed grooming and working around my horse. Besides, he enjoys having it done. He likes my company, and he shows it. I usually don't even turn him out when I clean his stall. I groom him and work around him in his stall even though he will cross tie. He likes my hands and trusts my touch. There is nowhere on his body I cannot touch. He knows I will not intentionally hurt him. Sometimes I do nothing but just sit and watch him graze. I believe I could lay down and sleep in his stall, and he would not mind or bother me.

If you cannot give of your time and yourself, DO NOT OWN A HORSE! They are expensive, yes. Nonetheless they are a lot less expensive than drugs or alcohol if you really want one, you can cut costs. Keep in mind, however, the more costs you cut, the more work you will have to assume—and the more your horse will literally count on you for his health and his well-being.

If you decide that the only way you can afford a horse is to rent a stall and do all the work, then consider this. You may have to feed the horse. That will mean *TWICE A DAY, EVERY DAY!* **No sleeping in on weekends.** A horse should be fed before 7 A.M. and before 6 P.M. That's pretty hard on evening plans, too. No matter how late you get in, even 3 A.M., you have to feed that horse before 7 A.M.!! That is when you have to remember how much you love and want him. There will be days when you don't feel good, but those chores still have to be done. You can't put it off until tomorrow like the dusting or vacuuming. You may have a cold, a cough, and a fever, but the barn chores still have to be done. The animals still have to be fed and cared for. Otherwise, you could end up with a sick horse and a good-sized vet bill just because you were lazy or not feeling 100 percent. I know what I am talking about. If you remember at the beginning of this story, I mentioned that my horse lived to be twenty-five years old. I had him from the time he was ten months old. He lived his entire life on my property and in my care. My new horse is on my property, too. Every morning and every evening I go down and take care of his needs. It is like having a child and raising it, except I truly believe a horse is much more appreciative than a child—more caring and more grateful. If you get your horse when he is young—say two to five years old—you can count on having him for twenty years! As long as your horse is healthy there is no reason why he can't live that long. That is a long time. The only other commitment in your life that will last that long will probably be your marriage. One of the hardest parts is trying to take a vacation and locating a reliable person to take care of your furry friend. I won't trust him to just anyone. On vacation I wake up automatically at 5:45, usually before the alarm goes off. I will call and check on him while I am gone. When we are out of town I will glance at my watch (which I leave set on home time) and say to myself, "They ought to be feeding right about now."

9

If you take care of your own horse, you may have to clean his stall—that means at least once a week. Every day or every other day is ideal and less work. The longer you let it pile up, the harder the work is and the heavier or wetter the manure is. Besides, the cleaner the stall, the cleaner the horse will be. You may also have to provide your own bedding. Around here we find that wood shavings work best. However, nothing is free. Don't cut corners and use sawdust. It is too dusty and may cause your horse problems. Don't use walnut shavings. These can cause harmful fumes when mixed with urine.

You may also have to schedule your own blacksmith visits and be there when he comes so you can hold the horse. In larger barns this is taken care of, and you are just billed. **You cannot let your horse's feet go. A horse is only as good as his feet and legs.** *NO LEGS, NO HORSE.* **If you care for nothing else,** *TAKE CARE OF HIS FEET!* The feet should be checked and trimmed every six to seven weeks. They should be checked and cleaned after every ride. They should be oiled no less than once a week. A dry hoof can cause you problems. They are the first to crack and chip. A white-footed horse may require even more care. The white hoof seems to break down faster than the black hoof. Whether or not you decide to shoe your horse is up to you. Trust your farrier's judgment. Depending on the condition of the trails where you ride, you may be able to allow your horse to go barefoot. This is the most natural way for the horse. Regardless, you have to check his feet AFTER EVERY RIDE. Don't let any chips go unattended. Remember to oil the feet to keep them supple.

You may have to plan your own veterinarian and worming schedule. Again, in larger more expensive barns the worming schedule is watched and posted, and you are billed. A worming program is very important for a healthy horse. Worms can make a horse very ill. He must also receive the necessary shots every year. Tetanus and influenza shots are the most important. Tetanus protects him from illness due to cuts and scratches which become infected. Wounds are susceptible to disease in a barn atmosphere. Just as you would do for your dog to keep him healthy, you have to have a regular shot and checkup program for your horse. If you keep him in a larger barn where many people trailer their horses out to horse shows, then many other shots may be required just to keep your horse healthy. Horses going to and from shows can bring many germs into the barn which would not usually be there.

You also have to have his teeth checked regularly. There are lots of things to consider in the health of your animal. He cannot do them for himself. It is up to you. Your veterinarian will guide you as to the proper care for your horse. **DO NOT BE AFRAID TO ASK QUESTIONS. NO MATTER HOW DUMB THEY SOUND! It is better to ask a stupid question than to have a sick horse.** After he has treated your horse for a while, your vet will know him just about as well as you do. He can give you advice and help over the phone without having to come out to see the horse. Your vet can be one of your best and most helpful friends.

RESPONSIBILITY

You have to remember this: horses require just as much care and thought as children. They cannot be stuffed into a closet and taken down only when you are in the mood to play with them. THEY ARE LIVING, BREATHING, CARING THINGS. They need attention just as you do. They cannot be allowed to stand indefinitely. They require regular exercise. They must get out of their stalls at least once a week. Three times is ideal. They must be allowed to kick up their heels and let loose all that pent up energy. How would you like to live every day of your life in a room ten feet by ten feet and see no one until you were fed twice a day. Think about that. You may as well put them in jail. At least prisoners get exercise time every day. A horse which is not properly exercised is also prone to health problems.

If a horse is well fed but not handled or ridden, it can sometimes become very rank. By that I mean it will test you. It will want to run and buck and jump, and some even become mean. There are some horses which can stand forever, and nothing ever bothers them. These are rare, especially among young horses. Older horses can stand and not be bothered, but it's not good for them to be idle because of their age. They need exercise to keep supple and healthy. Old bones become arthritic. They also need to be active to keep good circulation.

The younger the horse, the more exercise he will require to prevent boredom and to stay in shape. Muscles will not grow and develop without proper exercise. He may be well fed and even fat but have no muscle tone at all. Boredom in horses can cause bad stall habits like chewing, kicking, pawing, weaving, and cribbing. Remember, if you haven't been riding your horse regularly and for long rides, you must work him up to those longer rides gradually. You cannot let a horse stand for a month and then jump on and ride him for three hours. He will be sore and maybe even go lame. He will be more apt to pull a tendon or muscle. Also, you will be sore yourself. Like any athlete, to get into shape, you work at it slowly. Don't expect your horse to do anything you would not do yourself.

Here is one thing to keep in mind. **HORSES DO NOT THINK, THEY REACT!** A horse responds to outside stimuli. He can be controlled, and he can be made to respond, but he cannot be made to do anything he does not want to do without severe results or someone getting hurt. A horse responds to three things: **FOOD, FEAR, and FORNICATION.**

A horse is always interested in food or eating. A treat of food can win over just about any horse. It can help you train him, help you calm him, help you win his trust, and help you to get him to do something he is unsure of. I use food at first with a horse. After a while I eliminate the food and ask the horse to respond to my touch. I get him to come to me with food in the beginning. Later I remove the food and ask him to come to me just to be petted or touched. I won't always have food with me. I like when he comes to me because he knows me and trusts me. He likes my touch and wants the attention.

Fear covers a lot of territory. There is fear of getting hurt, fear of pain, fear of falling, fear of not eating, and fear of the unknown. A horse will panic quickly when he is afraid of something. That is how wild horses react. They run. They know that they are faster and can outrun most of their enemies. So they run first and look later. Once you have gained his trust and he completely trusts you and your judgment, he will be much less afraid of things. He will trust you and, therefore, have less fear. He will begin to know you will not let anything harm him. He will become braver because he knows you will not ask him to do anything which will get him in trouble.

Fornication is exactly what it says—sex!! Most geldings are over this problem once they are castrated. Mares are sometimes a problem during their heat cycles. At these times they can be very irritable. They can be nasty during grooming and sometimes do not like to be saddled. The mares cycle every twenty-eight days just like a woman. There are some stallions who are a problem all the time. They have nothing else on their minds. One friend used to say, "They have a testicle over each eye." Some stallions cannot be kept in the same barn as mares. They can actually be dangerous. DO NOT OWN OR HANDLE A STALLION UNLESS YOU KNOW WHAT YOU ARE DOING.

Please don't give your horse credit for being able to think and figure things out. There are some wonderfully intelligent horses, but they are exceptionally trained. The credit should go to the trainer not the horse. Horses are trained by controlling their outside stimuli, by realizing how they react to certain situations. Remember, some crazy thing might happen, and he will react entirely differently from the way you expect. Be aware that anything can happen. Always be ready to calm your horse and talk him gently through an unusual situation. I don't care how calm your horse is and how much "like a rock" you think he is. There will always be something which will cause him to "come unglued." Just remember that and be there when he needs you for strength to calm him. You may think I am crazy, that you are small and aren't influential to your horse. You are wrong. If your horse cares for you, you are a **GOD** in his eyes. You are ten feet tall and as strong as steel. My first horse would be startled by something in the pasture and run and hide behind me then peek out from behind me to see what it was. He felt that I would protect him! I was his **GOD.**

WINTER RIDING

As mentioned, I live in Ohio, and I used to have no arena to use in the winter. Here in Ohio we sometimes have severe winters. Nevertheless I did and still do ride all year. We are lucky enough to have access to well-maintained riding trails. I love the trails and prefer trail riding. Therefore, I have learned to cope and to protect myself and my horse.

When the weather was too severe to ride, I always took care of my horse. Sometimes I feel that the arena has spoiled me. Now if I don't feel like riding, I will just turn him out into the arena or lunge him. Before I had the arena to use, I would ride him more often because he could not go down trail by himself, and that was the only way he would get really good exercise. So the arena has both good and bad points. Regardless, I always go down to the barn and spend time with him whether I ride or not. **DON'T BE A FAIR WEATHER FRIEND. DON'T LET THE WEATHER KEEP YOU AWAY FROM THE BARN AND YOUR HORSE**. Make sure you spend time with him. Just go and groom him if nothing else. You are his best friend. He looks forward to seeing you and being with you. You can always turn him out into deep snow and let him roll. This is sort of like a winter bath. It does help to clean a lot of dirt out of the thick winter coat. A good grooming is almost as good as a work out. It stimulates the skin, helps circulation, and helps the muscles. A horse should not be left to just stand and get bored in the winter. He gets just as bored as you do, probably even more so because you have things to do and places to go. **If you are going to be a sometimes friend, a fair weather friend, then DON'T BUY A HORSE.**

I do not ride if the temperature is below eighteen degrees or if the windchill factor is below ten degrees. The windchill is the temperature combined with the velocity of the wind. It determines the actual temperature against exposed flesh. It is always colder when the wind is blowing. I do not ride if there is too much ice, but I do ride in deep snow. I have my horse's shoes pulled, and he goes barefoot all winter. This prevents unnecessary sliding with shoes. It also prevents snow-balling. That's when snow packs up inside the hoof. It is more likely to happen with steel

15

shoes. Snow-balling can cause a horse to slide and stumble. It's sort of like you trying to walk with a tennis ball attached to the bottom of you shoe. It hurts your arch and throws your foot all out of whack.

Now you may think I'm a sissy for not riding in colder weather, but I am not thinking of myself. I am considering my horse. I can dress for the bad weather. When a horse is ridden in severely cold weather it can harm him. Once he is warmed up by exercise and starts breathing deeply, he sucks that bitter cold air into his head and lungs. **This can cause his sinuses to bleed and can cause frostbite in his lungs. It can permanently damage your horse. You don't need that, and you don't want vet bills.** I have actually seen horses bleed from the nostrils in cold weather. I still can't believe people would actually do that to horses. It seems so cruel and stupid.

I have learned to dress for winter barn work and weather. I wear many layers of LOOSE clothing while working in the barn. I emphasize loose. Tight clothing is cold. To keep warm there must be air pockets between you and the outside air. As I get warm while working, I can take off one layer of clothing at a time. Sweating in the cold is just as bad as not dressing warmly enough.

I have many sweat shirts. I have thermal underwear. I have thermal hoods and knitted caps. I buy good insulated gloves and mittens. Yes, mittens!! Mittens are much warmer than gloves. I carry a pair of mittens down trail inside my jacket to keep them warm. If my hands get cold, I put the mittens on right over my gloves. When my hands get warm I take the mittens off and just use the gloves. If you try to save money and buy cheaper goods, that is what you will get. Buy the better items. Learn to stay warm, comfortable, and healthy. Don't care about how you look—just be warm and content. Worry about fashion and how you will look later. Your horse doesn't care if you are in style. He just wants you there with him. I have several pairs of snowmobile boots with washable liners. I have learned that your feet do sweat. When your feet sweat the liners become damp, and then your feet get cold. By having extra liners you can always have a dry pair of liners handy. I have a snowmobile suit I ride in. It is great! I wear it with a pair of light insulated underwear. I have learned to keep my hands and feet warm and dry and my head covered. **You lose over 80 percent of your body heat out the top of your head. Forget trying to look good, and just STAY WARM!** I hate to wear hats, but in the winter I sure-ly do it.

I do not blanket my horse in the winter. I did once, only to have him destroy an expensive winter blanket. Even when he was older, I found he was better off without a blanket. I do not show my horse. He stays clean as long as I keep his stall clean. I find he is healthier without a blanket. So I have to work a little harder to shed him out in the spring.

So what? Because I ride all winter long, I do not worry about him catching a chill because he has a heavy winter coat to protect him while we are out on the trails. He has been through twenty below zero weather without any problems and has been very content. I have even gone down to the barn in the middle of a severely cold night to check on him, only to have him look at me like I was nuts. My barn is warmer than most. It stays about fifteen to twenty degrees warmer in my barn than outside. It's probably due to all the warmth from the horses. I have been told that a horse will put out up to 2,500 BTUs of warmth per hour.

Another thing. NEVER PUT AN ICE COLD BIT INTO YOUR HORSE'S MOUTH! You wouldn't like it; why should he? Take the time to warm it in your hands, inside your jacket, or, if you have a heated water trough, in there. You horse can become hard to bridle if you don't take the time to care. If he refuses to open his mouth to take the bit, you'll wonder why.

Never let your leather dry out. **Remember, LEATHER WAS A LIVING THING. It must be kept moist and supple to remain strong**. Take proper care of your tack, and it will last indefinitely. Leather, if well cared for, does not wear out. The saddle you buy, if you choose it wisely, will last you your lifetime. I have been injured severely by tack failure. I know what I am talking about here. ***Always check your saddle and tack carefully.* Replace all worn parts.** Oil and care for your leather properly. Check all parts—reins, straps, bits. Look for loose parts and sharp objects, anything that may have worked loose with wear. Make sure nothing can injure you or your horse.

EXPENSES

Now to get into something serious about costs. . . .

Stable

Here in Ohio a loose stall or box stall will run you anywhere from $100 to $350 per month, per horse. The less money it costs, the more work you do yourself. However, remember this. For that money, here is what you get.

One box stall—approx nine by ten feet or larger
One tack box or place to store your gear
Use of one saddle rack
Use of the barn water to wash your horse (You may have to ask to do this if water is a problem.)
Use of the cross ties to work on your horse
Use of the arena to ride or work your horse (if there is one to use during bad weather)
Use of the hot-walker to cool your horse (if there is one available to you)
Use of the outdoor trails or riding ring (if they are available)
Use of the outside paddock or pasture to turn out your horse for exercise and fresh air
A place to store your horse trailer (if provided). Some barns charge extra to store your trailer.

That's all you get. This means they will clean, bed your stall, and feed your horse, and that is it. You will be expected to respect and care for this barn and property as if it were your own. Also, you must respect the rights of the other boarders. They are paying for the use of the facilities, too. Never bring people or children to the barn before checking with the owners. Never bring a dog to the barn before checking with the owner. Never allow people you know to visit the barn on their own or handle your horse without your permission or without letting the stable owners know.

NEVER HANDLE HORSES OTHER THAN YOUR OWN, and always, ALWAYS CLEAN UP AFTER YOURSELF! Make sure to turn off all lights and close all doors and gates before you leave. Be careful about the use of electricity. Think of it as if you were paying the bill. If your horse dumps in the arena, clean it up. If your horse causes large holes in the arena bedding, rake them over. You are not the only one using the arena, think of others. You would not like it if you were riding in the arena and had to work around large craters in the footing.

A lot of places charge you extra to turn your horse out for exercise; to remove and replace horse blankets; to hold your horse for the vet or the blacksmith; to ride or train your horse or work with your horse in any way; to groom your horse; to tend to sores and give any medication. You are expected to do all these things. After all, why would you own the horse if you never handled him in any way? If your horse is at all bad with the blacksmith or vet, it is a real burden on the stable owner to put up with this chore.

Veterinarian and Farrier

So you've bought your horse. It cost you X amount of dollars to buy him. It will cost you at least $100 a month to see that he is fed and his stall is cleaned. Now there are blacksmith (farrier) fees. Every six to seven weeks this horse will have to have his feet trimmed. His feet are just like toenails. They grow and have to be trimmed and filed. Otherwise, they will cause you and him problems. They can crack, chip, and peel just as your fingernails do when you don't care for them. Just to have them trimmed will cost between fifteen and twenty-five dollars. If he can go barefoot, fine. If not, shoes will be needed. To have new shoes put on will cost between forty and ninety dollars, more if special shoes are required or requested. To have old shoes reset will cost from thirty to seventy-five dollars. That's here in Ohio. You will have to check into prices in your area. You cannot let the feet go. **Remember what I said before: NO FEET, NO HORSE!**

Your horse can lose an eye (God forbid!), and you can still ride him. He can severely cut himself and carry an ugly scar, and you can still ride him. His ear can fall off due to severe frostbite—you can still ride him. Do you see what I am getting at? He can live with all these things but not bad feet! **If a horse injures his legs or his feet, he is out of commission and cannot be used!! He also cannot be sold!! NO FEET, NO HORSE! It is as simple as that!!**

Then there are veterinarian fees. A horse will have to have spring, summer, and fall worming at least. Some barns worm even more regularly than that. I have my vet worm my horses in the spring and fall.

19

In between that time I paste worm every five weeks. Each time your horse is wormed by the vet, it will cost at least fifteen dollars. Then there are the yearly shots. Each shot is usually around eight dollars to fifteen dollars apiece. As I mentioned before, he needs tetanus and influenza shots. Some barns may require other shots for health purposes. It depends on how many animals travel to and from horse shows. All kinds of things can be passed around at horse shows. You will also have to pay or share a barn call charge, which is extra over and above the exam and shots. The barn call charge helps the vet to maintain his vehicle, which he needs to do his job. Here at my barn the horses get rhino-pneumonitis, potomac horse fever, strangles, and we also get rabies shots in the spring. I believe it to be a good idea because we ride the trails in the park system. There have been reported cases of rabies in raccoons in this area.

Remember this: a horse is no good to you if he is not healthy. It is much easier to prevent diseases than to cure them. It is very easy to keep your horse healthy if you stick to a regular schedule for everything. A healthy horse usually stays that way with very little trouble. If you don't keep him healthy, you cannot even sell him if you decide to.

Tack and Grooming Supplies

Now there is your tack. I will not cover the costs for saddles. They are expensive. You will have to decide whether you want to ride English or Western. You should consider buying used rather than new tack. Some used tack, if well cared for, is just as good as, and sometimes better than, new. Besides, someone else has already broken it in.

Just to take care of your horse, you will need the following:

One curry	One hoof pick	A halter
One sweat scraper	Fly repellent	A lead line
One shedding blade	Hoof dressing or oil	Shampoo
One stiff body brush	Thrush medicine	
One soft face brush	Wound dressing of some sort for cuts, etc.	
One main and tail comb	Scissors or clippers	
A longe line (if desired)	A bridle with suitable bit	
A bucket and sponge	A caddy to carry everything for convenience.	

The cost of horse care products alone, without considering the cost of the saddle, can really add up. These are only the bare necessities. There are so many more you can use and will accumulate as time goes on. **DO NOT BORROW CLEANING EQUIPMENT FROM SOMEONE ELSE!!** Horses can acquire many skin problems which are contagious. Some of these are really hard to get rid of and can even be passed on to you! You don't need your horse picking up something from another animal because you were too lazy to buy a new brush or sponge. I have two horses, and I have a complete set of curries and brushes for each animal. Even though I know both horses are clean and healthy, I don't use one set of brushes for both. I just don't want to take the chance. I have seen skin problems pass through a barn like wildfire. I wash the brushes and curries at least three times a year—more often if possible. I just put them into the washer and agitate them on gentle with bleach and a good detergent. **DO NOT PUT YOUR BRUSHES IN THE DRIER!!** Just let them sit out in the sun and air dry. The drier can melt some brushes.

TO BUY OR LEASE A HORSE

After you have considered buying a horse, think about this. Look around for someone who owns a horse already. There are people who have horses and want to keep them but don't have the time to exercise them properly. They may be very happy to have someone, like you, keep their horse in top condition and keep it groomed and cared for. You can work something out with someone like this. Be sure to sign some agreement regarding this relationship. Be sure to cover the possibility of the horse being injured while in your care, and get it all down in writing. Be willing to sign a legal release which says that you take full responsibility for your actions and will not sue if you are injured while caring for this horse. You may not like the idea of these papers, but they protect both of you, not just the owner. It's best to have everything down in writing. Occasionally you'll find someone who will not want any money. However, more than likely the person will lease you the use of the horse for a monthly fee. Sometimes the vet and blacksmith bills will be theirs (unless the horse is injured in your care, in which case the vet bills may be yours). So with this agreement, you will be ahead. Also, if you decide you want to get out, you will not be stuck with trying to sell the horse.

You will have the use of a horse and the pleasure of it. You may be able to use their equipment. It may not cost you anything for vet or blacksmith fees. You may even be able to show the horse or take lessons on the horse with their permission. Most people agree readily to lessons, for the horse is being trained at the same time. The only thing to remember is this: the horse will not be yours. **A WORD OF WARNING HERE: Don't let yourself become too attached to this animal!** If the owner should decide to sell him, the new owner may not want to lend or lease the animal. You have to remember that this is a temporary arrangement and could end at any time. You could put into your lease paperwork that you are to be given first option to buy if the horse should be for sale.

KEEPING YOUR OWN HORSE

If you decide you still want a horse, but you decide you want to keep it and care for it yourself, here are some things you must know. First—and I speak honestly and from experience—you may think you know a lot about horses. **Believe me, YOU DON'T KNOW ENOUGH! I have been around horses all my life. I have known and learned from some of the best people in the area. Nevertheless, I soon realized just how little I really did know. You will learn together. Your horse will teach you as much as you teach him. NEVER, EVER, STOP ASKING QUESTIONS!!** Never stop seeking information or stop learning. Always keep an open mind and listen to any suggestions. You don't have to use them, but at least listen. You may just learn something new and worthwhile.

It's funny how much you learn about people just by listening. You learn quickly who knows the most and who thinks they know a lot. Also, the people who know the least are the ones who like to give the most advice. It is better and safer to ask a stupid question than to make a bad or fatal mistake.

Remember, a horse may seem big and invincible, they may seem rugged, some even look like they can thrive on neglect, BUT THEY CANNOT!! THEY ARE REALLY VERY DELICATE CREATURES FOR THEIR SIZE. Internally they are extremely delicate. They can develop serious problems in a very short time.

* * * PLEASE TAKE NOTE * * *

I have found, over the years, that it is sometimes very wise NOT to give too much advice. I have learned that no matter how much people may beg or ask for your advice and opinion about something, they may not always like your answer. They sometimes take it the wrong way and may think you are being nosy, you are opinionated, or you are interfering with their business. Everyone seems to think their way is best. Do listen, learn, and then do what you feel is best for you and your animal. Always depend on your vet and farrier for good advice.

Don't rely on someone you just met or know little about. You can get into a lot of trouble by giving what you feel is good advice, only to find out it went wrong. Tell the person to call the vet and ask him. Please don't give a horse shots or medication without the advice or instructions of a vet.

Getting back to keeping your own horse . . .

You will need a building for your horse. He will be better off in a box or loose stall. This should be sturdy and at least ten-by-ten feet in size. Twelve by twelve feet is even better. You will need storage space for at least fifteen to twenty-five bales of hay. You will need storage space for at least 100 pounds of good grain. Garbage cans—metal not plastic—will work fine. If kicked, metal will dent, but plastic will break. Just make sure your horse cannot get into the grain if he gets loose within the barn. If he overeats grain, it can cause serious problems. Have your grain stored in a separate room, which you can also use for a tack room for your saddle, bridle, forks, and shovels. You will need an area where you can cross tie your horse to clean him and dress wounds or work on his feet. A cross tie can be put inside his stall if you desire.

A barn should be no less than 100 feet away from any human dwelling. You will need a corral area at least thirty-by-fifty feet for exercise and or lungeing. You will need an area to store the manure. This should be at least 100 feet away from the barn if possible, to eliminate flies and odor. You will need a water hydrant which will not freeze in the winter if you live in the north. A water trough with a heating element works out nicely. It is also a handy place to warm a bit before putting it into your horse's mouth in the winter months. This is easier than warming it in your hands.

Get into the habit of checking your horse's manure. I don't mean this to sound funny. You can tell a lot about the horse and his health by looking at the manure. Healthy manure should be about the color of caramel or a little darker. It should be well formed in little balls. It should not smell rank or sour. It should be somewhat moist, not dry. If it smells really bad or sour, something is wrong. If it is very runny like a cow pancake, then something is wrong. If it is very dry, this is not normal. If it is very dark, almost black in color, this is not normal. It usually means something is missing in his diet. Check to see if there is any undigested whole grain in the manure. If there is, the horse needs to have his teeth checked. This usually means he is not chewing his grain entirely. There are a lot of things you can check by looking at the manure. A healthy horse has very healthy manure. Don't be afraid to pick up a ball of manure and break it open in your hands. It won't hurt you, and you can always wash your hands. If you ever see worms in you horse's manure do something about it right away.

24

Your barn should be well lit and airy. Keep your stall clean, and your barn will have little or no odors and fewer flies. Cleaning a stall is no easy chore. You'll need a sturdy shovel, a pitch fork, a rake, and a wheelbarrow. Rake aside any dry bedding which can be saved. Remove all wet bedding and manure. Clean all the way to the floor. Now sprinkle powdered lime on all the wet areas. Lime will keep the stall drier and help remove odors. Rake the old dry bedding into the urine pits and center. Place the fresh bedding on top. I usually bed a stall about four inches deep. This is about two wheelbarrows full of fresh bedding to start with, less when you are adding to the old. I usually pick out the stall when I feed daily. I have a manure fork and pick the fresh droppings after I have fed and the horse is busy with his grain. It keeps the stalls cleaner longer. We have found this to work best for us. However, you must make your own routine and find what works best for you.

I try very hard to keep my barn clean—not spotless, but clean. I try to always pick things up and put things away out of the way. I keep my aisleways swept and clear of debris. This is your workway. I have rubber mats down in my aisleways. When these are wet they can become slippery. I sprinkle sawdust bedding on them when they are wet. I don't want a horse or a person to slip and fall on them.

I dust away the cobwebs once a week, every other week when I am really busy. I scrub out the water buckets at least twice a month. I ask that my boarders try to help out when and if, they can, to keep ahead of the dirt and at least to ALWAYS clean up after themselves and put everything away. Because my barn is kept clean, there are few or no flies and no odors.

I try to make my work as easy as possible. I am always thinking of ways to avoid work whenever I can. For instance, after I ride my horse and clean him up, when I put him away, I take a carrot and a hoof pick into his stall with me. While he munches on his carrot treat, I clean and pick out his feet. That way the dirt is left in his stall, and I do not have to sweep it out of the aisleway—less work for me to do. If there is a stone in his foot, I put it in my pocket and put it in the trash when I am done.

A horse whose stall is kept clean will become a clean animal. He will select one area of his stall to be his toilet and will dump mostly in that area. He will use the rest of his stall for his bed, and he will stay cleaner. You will find that he will require less heavy grooming, and it will take less time to prepare to ride. Horses lay down more often when their stalls are clean. They rest or sleep more soundly when they lay down. If you enter my barn in midmorning you will catch three or four horses laying down—kind of a late morning nap. I have two horses that sleep so soundly they actually snore.

Clean your horse's water bucket at least once a week. Actually take it down and scrub it clean. A scum builds up on the sides of a water bucket, and it smells and should be scrubbed clean. Some horses are real slobs with their water buckets. Some wash their mouths out in their water, rinsing out a mouth full of grain and slobber. Some dunk their hay into it and make a kind of hay stew or soup. It can get really disgusting. Also, scrub and clean his grain bin once or twice a year. You do not eat from dirty dishes; why should he?

FEEDING YOUR HORSE

Feed your horse on a regular schedule. Remember, he depends on you for his food. You eat when you get hungry, and you get a headache or feel bad when you miss a meal. Well, he does, too. He cannot eat unless you feed him. Horses which are on a schedule should be kept on that schedule. They actually have tummy clocks which go off when it's feeding time. They know whether you are late or not. They will let you know when you come to the barn. They get very loud and complain. Some are just vocal, but others will kick or chew on the walls just to make noise. It is better for him to skip a meal than to be overfed.

Always make sure your grain is fresh and not too dusty or moldy. **Throw away anything you may question in any way. You don't need a sick horse or vet bills just because you didn't want to throw away a few dollars worth of iffy grain.**

NEVER EVER FEED YOUR HORSE MOLDY or ROTTEN HAY. You can tell if it is moldy. It will be brown or gray-black in color. It will smell musty or sour. When you break the bale apart it will smoke (sort of) as if it had been burning, and there will be a gray-like ashy look to the hay. A moldy bale got wet or was baled before it was thoroughly dry. That wet hay actually smoldered, became overheated, and rotted within itself. Wet hay sometimes will catch fire in a barn and cause a barn fire. Barn fires are very dangerous and costly. Always buy your hay from someone you can trust, or break apart a bale and check it thoroughly before you buy any of it.

If you are unlucky enough to have a barn fire —

DO NOT TRY TO PUT IT OUT!! DON'T EVEN WASTE YOUR TIME TRYING. DON'T BE FOOLISH. A BARN GOES UP VERY QUICKLY. IF YOU CAN, GET THE ANIMALS OUT. MOSTLY, GET YOURSELF OUT!!

Hauling hay is another heavy job. You can have your hay delivered, but it will cost more. You have to pay for the other people's work and time. To cut costs, most people haul their own. If you can buy it "off the field," i.e., before it is handled or put into a barn, it is cheaper still. You will need a pickup truck or large vehicle. You will need help. You will have to learn how to stack hay on a truck so it will ride steadily and evenly and not shift while traveling. If a load is not stacked correctly, the whole load can shift and fall off all over the highway. Bales may break open, and you will have one large mess as well as one large traffic jam and possibly an accident.

Bales are heavy, especially fresh bales. They run from forty-five to ninety pounds each, depending on their size and who bales them. Some farmers prefer large bales. Some bale them smaller. One standard-sized bale will last one horse for two days. Bales cost anywhere from $1.50 for the cheapest quality, to $5.00 or $6.00 apiece, depending on the type of hay and delivery charges. Again, these are Ohio prices. The price of hay is controlled by the weather and the amount of rain in a season. Too much rain is just as bad as a drought. If farmers cannot get into the field to bale the hay, it will go to waste. I feed my horses a Timothy grass-clover mixed hay, sometimes with a touch of alfalfa. I don't like anything too rich. The horses in my barn are pleasure horses. They are not bred or shown regularly. Therefore, they maintain well on a less rich hay.

Always have free salt handy. Free salt can be gotten at a feed store. Just ask for it. When you store your hay, sprinkle this salt on each layer of the bales as you stack them, especially if the hay is slightly green or seems damp or warm in any way. This will help the hay to dry out more quickly and help to eliminate the possibility of combustion. It is a good idea to set any damp bales aside and use them first rather than stack them with the other hay. We stack the first layer on edge to allow for better air flow.

One thing you must realize about needing hay. It can only be grown and harvested in the summer. That means that when you must haul hay, **THE WEATHER WILL BE HOT.** I must warn you to take great care. When you are hauling hay, drink plenty of water. Sports drinks such as Gatorade® are even better. You will have to replace the electrolytes you sweat out. AND YOU WILL SWEAT!! Be very careful not to get overheated and lightheaded. Be sure to wear long-sleeved light-colored shirts. We have taken to wearing old white or light blue dress shirts. The long sleeves protect your arms. If you do not cover your arms, you will soon look as if you have prickly heat. Keep your head covered. Eat lightly. We eat a lot of melons for water and chips or pretzels for the salt. If you try to eat normally or heavily, it can make you nauseous. The heat will give you a headache.

I cannot tell you how much your horse will eat. Each horse thrives differently on different food amounts. It depends on what kind of grain and hay you feed and how much he is worked or ridden. It also depends on his size or breed. Obviously, heavily worked horses will eat more than idle horses.

I feed mixed grain. I used to have my grain custom mixed rather than buy commercial mixes. My personal mix was made up of crimped oats as a base, quality sweet feed, shelled corn, and rolled barley. I have since found a commercial brand which is very close to my own and am now feeding that. You should feed less mixed grain than just plain oats, as they are more nutritious. Plain oats can cause some horses to be hyper. My horses are both "easy keepers." That means they eat very little to maintain good body condition and weight. On the average, a saddle horse will get two pounds (or quarts) of grain per feeding, totaling four pounds per day. I use a one pound coffee can as a measure. He will get two or three flakes of hay with each feeding (twice a day). He will drink five to ten gallons of water per day and more in hotter weather. Most people do not realize a horse will consume approximately one gallon of liquid each day for every 100 pounds of body weight. **Water makes up approximately 65 to 70 percent of the average 1,100 pound horse's weight—as many as 770 pounds!!** I do not feed pelletized foods. Some people like them, I do not.

I don't depend on hay for nutrition. I feed hay as a filler. It keeps the horses from becoming bored and gives them something to do. My horses get all their vitamins and nutrition from the grain. I do not skimp on grain. I also feed bran and vitamins twice a week. I feed loose bran mixed into the grain with the morning feeding. Then I feed a quality pelletized vitamin, soy bean meal (approximately $\frac{1}{2}$ cup), and loose mineral salt mixed into the grain with the evening feeding. I do this on Sundays and Wednesdays. Since I have been doing this, I have little or no colic problems in the barn. The bran works wonders, and the soy meal promotes good hoof and hair growth.

Always have salt and water available for your horse "free choice." By this I mean keep his water bucket full and a salt block in his stall at all times. He can use them at his leisure. If he eats the salt block too quickly, as some horses do, then put loose salt in his grain two or three times a week.

A flake of hay is the way a bale falls apart after you cut it open. Some people call them "slabs." When you cut a bale open you will know what I mean. Some horses will require less hay than others. If a horse seems to be wasting his hay, cut back. Give him only what he will eat in one meal. This will take a little getting used to. Some horses will need to have their hay moistened. Especially if they are allergic to dust or have "heaves." (Heaves is about the same as asthma in people—a breathing problem which makes it hard for a horse to breath without actually using his muscles to exhale.) Watering the hay is no problem. Keep a watering can near the stall to sprinkle the hay.

BRAN MASHES

I have recently started a new regimen with my horses. In one of my many horse magazines I found a good article about bran mashes. I tried it with my horses and discovered they really like it. I give them this once a week. It is a wonderful way to keep their insides clear or clean and keep everything moving properly. They really enjoy the mash, and I have a lot less to worry about internally.

The magazine gave several recipes for this mash, and I will include them here. You will need plain wheat bran. You can find wheat bran at your local feed store. A little bran goes a long way, so begin with only ten to twenty pounds. Bran does store well in a cool dry feed room or basement.

Some horses are not keen about plain steamed mash, so if you are making a mash for the first time, be prepared. Molasses, carrots, or cut-up apples or pears can be added to provide temptation. Some people add half a regular ration of sweet feed to the mash, and the horses never hesitate. After several feedings of mash and grain, they seem to eat the plain mash eagerly.

To make the mash, boil about two quarts of water. Fill a three-pound coffee can $\frac{3}{4}$ full with the wheat bran. Add two teaspoons salt and $\frac{1}{2}$ cup of molasses if you desire. Add any cut-up fruit or vegetables later because a mash full of apples is more difficult to stir that a plain mash.

Pour several cups of boiling water over the dry bran. Stir together with a sturdy spoon or sweat scraper. The sweat scraper works really well. Continue to add water until all the bran is moist. Be sure to stir all the way down to the bottom of the can, or you will have a layer of dry bran. When all the bran is moist, add a final inch or two of boiling water on top of the mash. This will be absorbed as the mash steams.

Now add apples, pears, or carrots. Cover with the plastic lid and let it steam. The coffee can will get hot as it steams. Wrap it in an old towel to protect your hands during transport. At the barn, take off the lid and check the temperature. It should be warm to the touch but not hot, or it will burn his mouth. Be sure to check the temperature in the center of the mash. Do this when you put it into the feed tub. Scrape out the can and give the mash a few stirs to dampen any dry bran. This will also help cool it. When you can hold the bran in your hand comfortably, it's time to serve the mash.

Rinse the cans thoroughly before taking them home and before the bran dries. Old bran remaining in the can will turn moldy and make your horse ill. Feeding bran mashes is more than a treat. Some vets recommend bran as a regular part of the diet because it provides a laxative effect. This is especially true in the winter when some horses don't drink enough water and are prone to colic.

Basic recipe: 3 pound coffee can $\frac{2}{3}$ full of wheat bran
                 2 teaspoons salt and $\frac{1}{2}$ cup molasses
                 2 quarts boiling water
                 cut-up apples or carrots or pears on top
For introducing your horse to mashes:
                 3 pound coffee can $\frac{1}{2}$ full of wheat bran
                 2 teaspoons salt, NO molasses
                 1 quart of sweet feed *
                 cut-up apples or carrots or pears on top
                 You can also add pieces of broken candy cane to the mash mix.
                 * Add sweet feed to steamed mash when you are at barn.

Here is something else to consider. There will be a time when you would like to go out of town on vacation. If you feed and care for your own horse, you will have to locate someone you can trust to take over this chore while you are gone. **Don't leave your horse's care to just anyone. This is your "best friend" we are talking about. Make sure your horse stays on a regular feeding schedule.** They can deviate a little. They can feed at seven instead of six as you do, but not much later than that. The stalls can go a little longer between cleanings, but the feeding schedule must be adhered to at all costs. It's not easy to find someone that dedicated. You will have to pay them something for their time and care. If you are able to have boarders in your barn along with your horse, you can trade them their board fee for taking care of the barn while you are gone. This usually works well because they are also taking care of their own animals. They would rather do this most of the time than have someone else care for their animals. They will also learn to appreciate you and what you do for their horses a little more when they have to do it themselves. When you come back they will remember that while they are snuggling deeper into their bed covers, you are already down in the barn feeding their horses.

FRIENDSHIP

Remember this: Your horse can become your very best friend. I will not tell you that you will never be hurt working around horses. I know better; I have been hurt seriously twice. You can avoid injury if you think before you do anything. **Remember, a horse reacts before he thinks. He is very intelligent, and he can think, but, when he is taken by surprise or startled or frightened, HE REACTS.** Usually, he reacts by bolting, spooking, or running. **When he is afraid, he may run over anything in his way. Including you!** If he trusts you, he will never do anything to hurt you intentionally. He will avoid hurting you at all costs. Again, if he trusts you, he will look to you for strength and help when anything crazy or unusual happens. If you are not afraid, then he will figure it cannot hurt him.

If you show fear, this will transmit directly to him, and he will be afraid. He may not even know why he should be afraid. He will just know that you are afraid, and it may hurt him, too. **IF YOU STAY CALM, CHANCES ARE HE WILL, ALSO. If you never ask your horse to do anything you would not do, he will not be hurt.** He will get to know this. He will learn that you will not allow him to be hurt, and he will have a deeper trust in you and your judgment. Remember, he does bleed and can be injured. He does not have a tough hide and is not covered by leather as many people believe. He is covered by skin just as you are, and he can be cut and scarred just as you can. If you always think of his safety, chances are he will not get hurt, and, therefore, neither will you. **If you guide him safely through a situation, then he will deliver you safely from it!!** When you ask him to do something unusual or difficult, he will try because he trusts your judgment.

DON'T BE AFRAID OR ASHAMED TO LOVE YOUR HORSE!!! It is only natural. Furthermore, if you love him, he will love and trust you. He will protect and probably die for you if he has to. That sounds a bit farfetched, I know. However, my horse actually placed himself between me and another horse one time. He took a kick that was aimed at me. If you get your horse young, as a baby, or from his first trainer before he is five years old, you can count on having him a long time. If he is sound, has good lungs, legs, and feet; and has a strong heart; he could live to be thirty years old as long as you take good care of him. There are not many things in life which will stay with you that long. Some marriages don't last that long.

NEVER LET ANYONE TEASE, TORMENT, OR MISTREAT YOUR HORSE!! Correct or reprimand your horse when necessary. Don't let him develop any bad habits which could become dangerous. Don't play with your horse as if you are another horse. He will soon start treating you like another horse. Have you ever seen horses play together? They play very rough! They nip each other, strike out at each other, bump and rub up against each other. That is how he will start treating you—very rough. He has to understand that he must treat you only with respect and very gently. I remind you again, never ask your horse to do anything stupid, dangerous, or crazy. If you would not do it, don't ask him to do it!! When you ask him to do something new or different, you may have to ask him two or more times. He will think about it, maybe even hesitate, but he will do it because he knows you will not put him in any danger.

TRAIL RIDING

I am basically a trail rider. I do not totally enjoy arena riding. I will work in an arena to adjust problems and perfect commands and movements. Nonetheless, I love the trails and nature in general. Also, I will school my horse and work on his commands while I am on trail.

We are blessed here in Ohio. We have what is called a Metropolitan Park System. It is referred to as the "Emerald Necklace" because it completely encircles the city of Cleveland with the park system. Within the park system we have over eighty miles of well-maintained bridle paths and bike trails. There isn't a nicer place to own and enjoy a horse. We are very lucky. Cuyahoga County has more horses and horse owners than most places.

The average person does not realize how a horse will react to things. Most people who come down into the park have no idea what a horse will tolerate. They think of a horse as if he were Mr. Ed. They don't realize a horse will "freak out" at just about anything.

We horse people refer the city apartment dwellers as "cliff-dwellers." They spend all their time in an apartment, living stacked on top of one another in their cement cliffs, and only get out to enjoy the outdoors on weekends. Then they converge on the park, and all heck breaks loose.

I have had a person throw a Frisbee between my horse's legs. I have had them drop fire crackers under my horse. Then there are people who drive by you and want to see your horse. They park alongside the road and wait for you. When you approach the car they fling the door open in front of your horse's face and then wonder why your horse tries to climb a tree.

There are always people walking along the bridle paths. They want their kids to see and pet a horse. They are not used to horses. They all start walking up to the horse. They get excited and may run towards the horse. One time I had a family approach me. They had a yappy little dog on a leash. They had a baby in a stroller. There were balloons tied to the stroller. There were three excited kids all yelling. My horse is standing there with eyes and nostrils as big as soup dishes, wondering if he is going to die. I had to explain that my horse has no idea what a stroller is and that it would not be a good idea to get the baby too close because it might get stepped on.

My horse will put up with a lot, but there is a limit. He does love kids. I have known him to walk into a group of kids and drop his head just to be petted. One time he walked into a group of kids and did this. There was a family there with some very small children. I felt Bandit tense and wondered what was wrong. I looked down and saw that a young child of about three years old had wrapped her arms around his back leg and was hugging him with all her might. Bandit did nothing; he just became tense. He would not move. I had to get the mother's attention and ask her to carefully remove her child so it would not be hurt. She was amazed at how quietly the horse stood. I was, too.

There are other dangers down trail. Some people will go out of their way to excite or frighten horses. One time I was riding along the river beach. A woman had a rather large dog loose and was playing with him. The dog tried to stalk my horse. I asked her to please call him and put him on a leash. She ignored me. I told her that my horse would kick and may harm the dog. She made some nasty remark. I told her there was a leash law and I would not be responsible if her dog was injured. She finally called her dog. On the way back from our ride she was still there. When she saw me coming she released her dog. I believe that it was on purpose. The dog immediately started after my horse. I gave the horse his head and kept watching the dog. My horse kept sight of the dog and kept circling to avoid him. When the dog charged us from behind, my horse gave one sharp kick. He caught the dog directly in the head, and the dog fell dead without making a sound. The girl was all upset. I told her that I had warned her previously what could happen. I then told her that I would report the whole thing to the rangers when I returned home, and I did. The rangers said that they had received no report but took my information. I decided the girl must have realized she was wrong and had done nothing about it.

Another time when I was riding, I had trouble with motorcycles. We have river fords in the park. Nearly all these have been replaced by bridges, but there are still a few left. These fords flood when the river is high, and the authorities close the roads to keep the cars off them. When the roads are closed I will ride over the fords instead of through the deep river. I was riding over a ford one day, and it was partially covered with water. I heard a motorcycle come up behind me. I didn't pay much attention to it until he tried to pass me on the river ford. He was trying to pass me on the right in the middle of the ford, and he was making my horse nervous. I told him it was not a good idea and said he could be seriously hurt if my horse spooked and tangled with his bike. He thought I was being smart and said some unmentionable words. I told him I was being nice and didn't want him or us to be injured. I suggested that he wait until we were out of his way. His two friends stayed well back and did not try to bother us. He finally got the message when my horse moved over and almost crowded him off of the ford and into the river.

People have no idea how dangerous a horse can be. A thousand pound horse can do a lot of damage to a car or a bike or a baby stroller. Horses have no intention of hurting you, your child, your dog, or your car. They just want to be left alone. They do not want to be hurt or bothered. They just want to enjoy the park and their exercise, just as you do. As big as they are, they are easily frightened. They believe that someone running up to them intends to hurt them. They think a balloon or umbrella or flapping clothing will eat a horse alive!

If you want to pet a horse, ask. Most of us will say yes. Don't run up to a horse. They think you mean them harm. Walk up quietly. Don't approach them with balloons flapping in the breeze. Don't walk up to them with a walking cane or stick in your hand. Don't throw things at them. Don't blow your horn or shout or race your engine just to see what they will do. I have had so many people do this. They never stick around to see if I was hurt or thrown or trampled. They think it's funny, and they don't care. People like that are sick and stupid.

One time I was riding my first horse, Comanche, near a picnic area. A small boy left his picnic and came running up behind Comanche, all excited. My horse, not sure what was going on, became excited and went into a Levade-type pose (a sit-squat slight rear position) and started to back up. He was backing right toward the child. I hollered at the child to go away and tried to calm down the horse. Once I got the horse under control and calm, I walked him over to the people. I explained that I was sorry for scaring him and asked if he would like to pet the horse. I told him that he had frightened the horse when he ran up behind him. I told him to always approach a horse where he can be seen and to do it slowly and quietly. I do not want people to be afraid of my horse, especially not children. If I had left, this child would have remembered only a bad experience with a horse. I do not like that. He got to love on my horse, and when I left he was all smiles and waved good-bye.

Trail bikes and in-line skates can lead to other unpleasant experiences. Some people who own trail bikes think they should be allowed to ride them on our trails. When they approach, they do not even slow down or try to get off the trail. They think horses see bikes all the time and will not go ballistic or try to climb a tree. They even try to ride between two horses. Horses and bikes just don't mix.

Riding with Others

When you ride down trail with other people, use common sense. If you are not used to riding with others, you must remember that horses are herd animals. One horse will do what another horse does. When you are ready to leave, make sure everyone else is ready. If you take off before the other people are ready, they will have trouble mounting if their horses take off to be with yours.

If you want to lope, ask if the other people mind. Their horses will want to run, also. Maybe they do not want to run. When you cross a river, make sure your horse does not splash and drown all the other riders. When you come up out of the river, don't let your horse run up the bank if the other horses are in the middle of the river. They will begin to run to catch up and may fall in the river and injure themselves or their riders.

Don't crowd on the trails. String out, and make sure your horse doesn't push another rider into a tree or other obstacle. When you come to a road, wait for the other horses. Cross the road all together. It is safer. If your horse tends to kick, tie a red ribbon to his tail as a warning to others. They will keep their distance.

Take care of each other on the trail. If there is a problem, warn the people behind you of what is ahead: a bottle on the trail, glass, a large hole. Always look for anything which could cause your horse to be injured or frightened.

Trail riding is fun. It's a wonderful way to get good exercise and to enjoy nature at the same time. However, be careful. Nothing is perfect. Always be aware of what is happening around you. Be sensible, cautious, and thoughtful of others. A good habit to get into, also, is to carry proper identification with you whenever you ride. Carry it on your body, not on your horse. If you are thrown or get separated from your horse, you, not your horse, will need the identification. Make sure to put medical alert information with your identification: your blood type, allergies, etc. Carry a quarter so you can make a phone call and a few dollars in case there is someplace to buy a drink. Carry a hoof pick and some leather ties for emergency equipment repairs. Carry a bandanna. This makes a good emergency bandage or, heaven forbid, a good sling.

Don't expect trouble, but be prepared. I have been hurt while riding. I know what can happen. I ride every week, sometimes three or four times a week. I love to ride trail and enjoy it whenever I can. I cannot seem to convince the people in my barn to carry identification and emergency equipment. I don't know why. Maybe they think it can never happen to them. WRONG!!!!

SAYING GOOD-BYE

This is a subject no one likes to talk or think about. Nevertheless, I feel I must cover it. There may be a time when the only decision you can make for the wellbeing and comfort of your horse is to "put him down." By that I mean, you must have him humanely destroyed or put to death. I can talk about this subject very truthfully because I have had to say good-bye to my sweet "OLD MAN."

My Morgan gelding lived a long happy life with me on my property. I brought him home in the back of a pickup truck when he was ten months old. I trained him, broke him to trail ride, and took care of him all his life. When he was twenty-three I noticed he was having trouble with his hind quarters. Upon examination it was decided that his right rear stifle was weak and showing signs of old injuries. The stifle is equivalent to the human knee. He was stumbling more often, and once he even fell, going head-over-heels with me on his back while we were down trail. He was unable to recover when he started to fall, and he was actually afraid of hurting me. After he fell, when he saw I was all right he was afraid to come to me. When I was finally able to catch him he was very apologetic.

I noticed that he was having trouble getting up once he was down. My biggest fear was that I would go down to the barn and find him thrashing desperately, unable to get up on his feet. It was then I decided to let him go with what dignity he still had left. My vet actually thanked me for making the decision. He had treated him since he was three years old. He said, "I could not have stood to see him deteriorate and go down hill. I'm so glad you decided to do what you did."

This may be the most difficult decision you will ever have to make. **Remember, *don't think about yourself at this time*! Think of your animal, your true friend. Do what is best for him.** In time you will get over your loss and your hurt. The pain they are having only ends when you let it end. Don't let your horse suffer or hope that he will just die naturally so you won't have to make that final decision. Put yourself in his place. Try to feel his pain. He deserves better treatment. He gave you a lot of fun and happiness. Do as much for him. He deserves all the comfort and dignity you can give him.

I must add this even though it is not all that nice. For a horse to die naturally is not that pleasant. There are many reasons for a horse to die. Most of them are not as fast or painless as a massive heart attack. Most are organ problems which can take a long time to kill the horse; many hours, maybe many days. In the mean time, **the people who are taking care of this animal are suffering just as much as he is. You, being the owner, have the option to stay away and not watch. The people who take care of the animal have to be there every day. They also have other animals in the barn who will become very upset by another horse being in pain.**

Not everyone has the option of isolating a sick or dying horse in another barn. They may not have that kind of room. **If a horse is in a great deal of pain, he could become wild with that pain. He could thrash, kick, bite, and bang into walls. He could become uncontrollable. Just think of 900 to 1,200 pounds out of control with pain! He could severely hurt someone who is trying to help him.** He may have to be put down inside his stall, and then there is the problem of getting a dead horse out of a stall. They may have to tear down a wall just to get the body out. Winching a dead horse out of a stall is not a pleasant task or sight. These are all things you, as the owner, have to consider. Be nice enough to your animal and the people who look after him to let him go peacefully, while you still have control of the situation.

It is a very quick and very painless process. When done properly by a veterinarian, it is done by injection. The horse does not suffer, and he will feel no pain. I was there for my horse. I held him while the vet gave the shot. The animal is actually dead before he hits the ground. It is that quick. The medication goes directly to the brain. It stops all brain function. **If your furry friend could talk, he would thank you!!**

BUYING A HORSE

Now, where should you get your horse? Spend as much time as possible around a barn with a good reputation—a barn which has clean stalls, healthy-looking horses, and level-headed people. When you have gotten to know them well enough, and they know you and how you feel about horses, confide in them. Ask their help to look for a healthy sound horse. Don't look for color or breed. Decide how you want to ride, English or Western. Don't turn down looking at a horse because you aren't familiar with his breed. Look for disposition, temperament, and good health. Color is the last thing to consider. You want a horse you can love, trust and ride. Why buy a horse of a certain color just because you always wanted it, only to find out that he kicks, bites, won't canter without a fight, or won't cross a river without laying down in the middle?

Never buy a horse without having a veterinarian check him very thoroughly. Then buy him only on a trial basis. Get this in writing: You have the option to return the horse for a full refund within the first month if, upon thorough examination, your vet finds him to be lame or not sound or if he has anything wrong which did not show up upon your first examination. You would do that much if you bought a car. If the seller will not agree to this, he is either hiding something or is not a good person to deal with. He should be wanting the best home for the animal, also. Have your vet x-ray his legs. Also, and this is not unusual, a horse may have been drugged to hide a painful injury so that he will move soundly. This is done all too often. During this trial month any drugs will wear off, and the injury will show itself when he feels pain again.

NEVER BUY A HORSE WITHOUT RIDING HIM!! Never buy a horse which is all saddled and ready when you get there. Ask yourself, what are they trying to hide? What is it they don't want me to see? Make sure you see the horse in his stall and at his worst. Watch him being groomed, saddled, and bridled. Look for any bad habits. Pick up and touch all four feet. Make sure his legs can be handled. Mount and ride him without help. Make sure he will load into a trailer. If you hope to show him, make sure he will stand for clippers.

THE RIGHT HORSE

I want to add this at this point. Please use common sense when you decide to buy a horse. If you buy a horse because he is beautiful or just because he was cheap enough and you could afford him, this is very stupid. You should chose a horse because you are right for each other. If your horse is "gorgeous" but you are afraid to ride him, then he is a useless expense, and nobody thinks he is gorgeous except you. Don't "outhorse" yourself.

When you go out to see your horse, you should be excited but relaxed and happy. You should be very calm and content around your horse. It should not make you nervous or upset in any way. Your horse should be your friend, your tranquilizer, your Tylenol®. You should look forward to being with him, not only to ride him, but just to be around him. If you are nervous about being with him in any way or are afraid to work him or ride him, then you have no business owning him. There are too many nice horses out there to be stuck with one you can do nothing with.

Eventually your nervousness will transmit to your horse. He will not understand why you are jumpy or nervous around him. He will think there is something wrong—that there may be something he should be nervous about. He will begin to NOT TRUST YOU.

You should be able to touch your horse anywhere on his body, and he should trust you and your touch. He should look forward to you and your touch. He should trust everything you do and should know you will not hurt him. He should relax when you are with him and relax when you are on his back. You should be able to ask him to do anything and expect him to do it.

REMEMBER THIS: IF YOU ARE AFRAID TO RIDE OR WORK WITH YOUR HORSE, THEN YOU OWN THE WRONG HORSE. A horse should be a means to relax and enjoy yourself. If you cannot do this with your horse, then you are just throwing a lot of money away every month. Why pay to be afraid or miserable? What a waste of time and money!

You would not stay in a marriage if you felt that way. Don't put yourself in that position with your horse. Call it quits. GET A DIVORCE! Then go out and find yourself another quieter more trusting and loving horse. You will be so much happier.

IN CONCLUSION

As I mentioned before, I had my first horse for over twenty-five years. I got him when he was ten months old. I thought I knew a lot about horses, especially since I first started with horses when I was six years old. I was trained by a sweet old man who taught me to ride like an Indian. At first I spent weeks cleaning and oiling tack. I knew all the parts of a saddle and bridle and how to take them apart and put them back together. Then he assigned me a horse and a bridle and asked me to groom and take care of the horse as if it were my own. When I could ride well, he finally gave me a saddle to use. As it turned out, I still prefer to ride without a saddle.

I have been learning ever since that time. My first horse turned out great, which is quite an accomplishment since he only learned from me. I am not a qualified or professional trainer. He was a loving trusting animal. There were only a few things he would not do, but these were my fault. Furthermore, they were nothing I couldn't live without. As I said, I trained him myself. I knew little or nothing about training, but I could not afford a good trainer. The only way I could afford to own a horse was to keep it and care for it myself. I did not have the extra money to pay board in a stable. I just used common sense and treated him like he was a person. I just figured if I wouldn't like something, why should he?

He was a super horse—a safe trustworthy trail horse. He was traffic safe and levelheaded. However, he did not like to back up, he was never in a horse trailer, and he would not stand for clippers. Other than that, you couldn't ask for a better or more loving horse. I never had the use of a trailer, so I could not train him to load and unload. Fortunately, I never showed and had wonderful trails right by my home, so I never had the desire to trailer and ride elsewhere. I only cut his bridle path and never trimmed his face hair, so the fact that he did not like clippers was no big deal. He trusted people, and if he really liked you, he was as loving as a loyal dog. He was never seriously ill. He was never seriously lame. He loved long rides and enjoyed new adventures down trail. He would do anything I asked of him with a little encouragement.

I never had a riding lesson in my life. I'm a good rider but not a polished rider. About five years before I lost Comanche I had a good friend ride him, and it was then that I found out just how well he was trained. She could ask him to do things I never knew he was able to do—change leads, side pass—all those finished movements. As it turns out, I was asking him to do all these things all along. I just did not realize it. We were so in tune to each other he would do them automatically. If I wanted him to do something or move a certain way, he would do it. Now that I have had a few lessons, I now the cues to give to ask a horse to do certain things. I was able to do these things all along, but I didn't realize I was doing them. It's amazing what a few lessons can do! It took a schooled rider on my horse to make me realize just how much I had actually taught him.

It's amazing how Comanche would pick up on my moods. When I felt good, he felt good, and I knew I was in for a good ride. When I was down, it was as if he understood. It was almost as if he was saying, "How can I help?" When I was sad and just wanted to be around him, he was extra loving. It was a really great relationship, a great friendship. He nursed me through the death of my father and my mother's death and was there whenever I needed a shoulder to cry on. Now I am finding that I have the same close relationship with my new horse. It may even be a closer friendship because I have more time to spend with this horse. I worked full time when I had my first horse. I don't have to work now and have more time to spend taking care of my horse and the barn. I am also older and a lot wiser now, much more comfortable in life. I don't have the hang-ups of youth and youthful competition. I have matured enough that I appreciate my horse more. I don't have to prove anything anymore. Things which were important to me then, I now realize are not all that important. I only wish I thought then as I do now. I would have enjoyed my first horse even more. I sometime wish I could stand them side by side so I could compare them. They would have been wonderful together. I believe they would have liked each other and been good friends.

I wish people could give friendship willingly and without compromise or questions the way animals do. Animals are totally incapable of lying. It's the old "what you see is what you get." They are just what you see, nothing else. They do not cheat or pretend. They love openly and honestly. They are not affected by greed, lust, vanity, or pride. They are loyal and loving. They hate and distrust only if you give them reason to. If you hurt, starve, or abuse them, then they have reason to distrust. But, why would you? They are always there, waiting just for you and your care and affection. I honestly believe I care for and desire the company of animals over and above that of most people I know. I truly believe my horse is my **best and closest friend** along with my dog and, of course, my husband. **GOD** bless my sweet and caring husband—for he is stuck with a HORSE NUT!!!

SO, DO YOU REALLY WANT THAT HORSE?

If you still do, great!! More power to you!! It's a wonderful experience. Remember, though it's a lot of work, and you can't let it pile up like those dirty dishes and just get to it tomorrow. Never neglect your horse. Never put him away hot or dirty, no matter how late you are. Remember, if you're late for a date and short cut your horse, you could come out to a very sick animal the next day. You may be on time for your date, but you may suffer with your horse just because you didn't want to take time to do what you should have done. Cut your ride short if you have to or be late for your date. Never short change your horse. He didn't arrange your schedule, you did!! *If you do not have time for your horse, you should not own him*!! **He did not choose to be your horse. You chose to own him. He owes you nothing! So if you take the time to care and show him how special he is, you will be rewarded in ways you will not believe!!**

GOOD LUCK TO YOU—AND HAPPY RIDING!!!

—◇—◆—◇—

REASONS YOU SHOULD CALL
THE VETERINARIAN

The following ten instances are cases when you should call your veterinarian unless you are highly trained and skilled with horses.

1 The horse has a temperature of 102° or above.

2 In cases of severe colic.

3 In cases of deep wounds or wounds near the joints.

4 Your horse is very lame or does not respond to your treatment for a slight lameness.

5 The horse slobbers and appears to have trouble eating his grain.

6 The horse has a skin disease which does not respond to treatment.

7 In all cases where the horse has not responded to the treatment you have given him.

8 The horse has a yellowish discharge from the nose.

9 The horse stops eating or has not drunk any water for more than one day.

10 You feel there is something wrong with the horse, but you are not able to tell what the trouble is. (Trust your judgment here. No one knows your horse better than you do.)

11 A mare has trouble foaling (delivering a baby).

NEVER BE AFRAID TO CALL IF YOU HAVE ANY QUESTIONS no matter how stupid the question may sound to you. Better safe than sorry. The vet would rather you ask that "stupid question" than have serious complications with the horse.

If you have had the vet for a long time, he will know the horse just about as well as you. He will know when something is "not right" with the animal. When you explain the situation to him, you may hear him say, "That's not like Champ" (or whatever the horse's name is). In many instances the vet can help you over the phone and may not even have to come out to the barn.

REMEMBER THIS: If the problem is serious, you can lose a horse in a matter of a few hours, and by lose, I MEAN DEATH!!

BEST WISHES AND HAPPY HORSEPLAY TO ALL OF YOU!!!

JAN D

Remember to hug your horse for me!